Horizon's Place And Time Meet
A Collection of Poetry

Cara E. Moore

Copyright © 2006 Cara E. Moore

All rights reserved.

ISBN: 0955539404
ISBN-13: 9780955539404

DEDICATION

This book is dedicated to the love of poetry, the perfume essence of writing. It is writing at its most powerful and concentrated. To my son Christopher who also shares the love of reading and poetry.

Table of Contents

Introduction	2
Horizon's Place And Time Meet	3
The Emerging Pioneer	4
The Wick	5
A Cheerful Canvas	6
The Web	7
Autumn Morning	8
Destiny Within	9
The Step Beyond	10
Flights of Freedom	11
Parallel Worlds	12
Lullaby	13
A Writer's Locket	14
Buffer Zone	15
Denial	16
Currents Within	17
Breeze	18
Shackled Meditation	19
Burnished Christmas Memories	20
The Fallen Tree	21
Heart Reality	22

Cara E. Moore

ACKNOWLEDGMENTS

I would like to acknowledge the publication of select poems in this edition in journals and online and performances at events and as an art form in the Burien Arts Gallery and as cards and posters.

Introduction

Poetry Statement

Horizon's Place And Time Meet is a collection of poems that deals with "coming of age" issues, and the struggle to maintain dignity throughout this process. From idealist beginnings, to the harshness of being judged before one is established. To define and decide what is acceptable as a condition for existence. Each event and remembrance molds and defines one's perception of life. Stepping back and asking, "Is this who I am?" Or "Is this who others have decided I am?" and what is their or my own motivation for this conclusion.

HORIZON'S PLACE AND TIME MEET

In my dreams, I'm a weightless crusader.
I motion and move towards my desired destination.
Soaring, I survey my own horizon -- all
the places I have been and would like to go.
These moments are captured in the morning's quiet
 before the grounded world pulls me back.

I carry my vision throughout the day,
into my dreams, flowing over into early morning
I move away again with the dawning light.
This is where I exist.
I step into the daylight still clothed in
dream's glowing costume.

Refusing to be contained within the mail; worn
only in half days of nights before dawn, my
dreams seep through the openings, creating a
runway of light towards the place where
horizon and time will meet.

By Cara E. Moore © 2004

Mumbles, Swansea, Cara E. Moore © 2006

THE EMERGING PIONEER

I see the reflection in your eyes
of understanding and curiosity.
I see your emergence into
the world; the mingling results,
of impulses and impressions enacted.

Like the pushing forth of a seed,
formed, but hidden, searching and
Reaching to surface into the light.
Your mind is full of play.
Created shadows beckoning to be followed.

A pioneer, on a road not yet taken;
Its experience and meaning unrealized.
A voyage that many have taken before, but one
whose traveled path is forged individually.

Each traveler brings with oneself a
Perception of accumulated experience.
The passing on the baton of knowledge.
The stretching out of arms to form,
a bridge, of continuity and co-existence.

By Cara E. Moore © 2005

"Duke", St Fagan's Cardiff, Wales Cara E. Moore © 1997

THE WICK

There is a sort of defiance
in the preserving of the thread
of integrity in one's existence.
It is the cupping of one's heart around
the flame of the human spirit.

Despair and treachery are enemies
of the autonomy and identity needed to exist.
Treachery works with the same compulsion of
a pair of scissors, snipping at
an isolated stray thread.

Despair descends with the looming stillness
of a candle snuffer extinguishing a flame. It
surrounds the flame and cuts
off its air, hope.

The light of hope that warms us
with the strength of well-being
and gives us the capacity
to endure, in completeness.

By Cara E. Moore © 2004

A CHEERFUL CANVAS

The cleaned grate looked bare.
Like the focused solitude of a
white canvas, a solid foundation.
The cleared ash stood cooling, in
a silvery-hued metal bucket at the
hearthside, insignificant.

The action of clearing the ash,
the lifting of lint from a filter.
Its substance, the meshed detail
of impressions consumed and set aside.

The beginning of a fire starts as
something fragile, the sputtering of
sparks igniting fuel into illumination.
From the cast-iron appearance of coal
springs the incandescence of warmth. Its
cheeriness, being in the reaching out to
those that gather around its glow.

By Cara E. Moore © 2004

1950's Kitchen, St. Fagan's, Cardiff, Wales, Cara E. Moore © 1997

THE WEB

There are connecting warp threads that form the
spatial definitions of human identity. These weave
patterns are interlaced
into one's own individual design.

Yet, like a web,
individual threads are fragile and can
be shorn from their foundations. Like
the fragile life
they reflect in their patterns.

Preserving the knowledge of the weaver
enables us to pick up past threads
that bind and connect us each as a people.
To continue the weaving of an existence in
an unique pattern of completeness.

By Cara E. Moore © 2004

AUTUMN MORNING

The Autumn morning lights seems brighter than Summer.
Milk bottles with cream wait underneath their silvery foil.
The clinking of the milk float moves away.
The dying embers of the banked up coal fire, are like the
Morning light against the gray sky background.

I empty the full ash pan into the metal bucket and
Gingerly place pieces of fresh coal on the embers.
I place the piece of shield-like metal across the
Fireplace opening to catch the fire.

The electric kettle clicks off. Hot water
for strong tea is ready. The mug warms my hands.
The remaining water will be taken upstairs
For a morning freshening up.

The warmed air of the electric fan heater in the bathroom
Mixes the cold dampness, forming pockets of warm and cold.
The fire downstairs hisses as it gains strength.
The plastic that covers the bathroom window billows
In and out with the force and gusts of the wind.

Dressing quickly in many layers, I go downstairs and
Remove the metal shield. The fire is alive and growing.
It is still early. I refill the kettle for another cup
Of hot tea and pour Muesli into the bowl. Dashing milk
In the tea and on the cereal, I put the milk in the fridge
To keep it from freezing in the unheated kitchen.

Looking out of the kitchen window I see the coal shed and the
Yard shared with the next door in the rows of miner's cottages.
It would be time to get more coal soon. The leaves of
The trees rise up the hill in back in bright hues.
A few are scattered in the yard and on the road that runs
Between the yards and the coal sheds at the back of the houses.

I bring the tea and cereal back into the warmth of the
Front room and switch the radio on. The radio and the
Hissing of the fire keep me company. This is the time
Of day that I can call my own. Nobody expects me to be up.
I count the change on the top of the cupboard for a bus
Trip into town for shopping and a job interview.

In the early morning light the day is becoming a reality,
The fire is gathering strength and I collect together the
Pieces of routine that strengthen me for world outside.

By Cara E. Moore © 2004

DESTINY WITHIN

I feel like a future butterfly wrapped in a cocoon.
The unique cocoon of one's own individuality.
Each butterfly starts out as a caterpillar, just as
Each person starts out as less of what they will become.

There is a sense of loss, of something not yet grasped;
Yet there is an inner knowledge of the goal.
To reach one's dreams one must fortify oneself against
The intensity of criticism, to buffer the torrents of
Rain that riven the shell of one's being.

To be a butterfly one must go through a transformation
And with change there is isolation.
The isolation of the cocoon.
The inner longing realization of what is to come.

By Cara E. Moore © 2005

THE STEP BEYOND

I have cried a thousand tears.
Each tear like a trickle of hot oil running down my heart.
I cry out in pain; the sound echoes down the corridors of my being
The instinctive changing forces of nature; the
Force that instills survival.
The need to survive as intact as possible.
The walls of constriction of my old self dig into my insides
And causes the formation of a new vulnerable exterior.
I step away from the empty shell like the Metamorphosis
Of an insect that has outgrown its old shell.
The bursting forth of a new being,
Soft and vulnerable, but a continuation and
A step beyond the shell left behind.

By Cara E. Moore © 1987

FLIGHTS OF FREEDOM

Freedom is the feeling of unencumbered living. Not
void of responsibility, but the absence of an excessive
burden of one's mind and spirit.

Dreams bridge the gap between reality and goals. Sometimes
even veiling an underlying reality that carries on. Mercifully
spared from the actuality.

Freedom and dreams are intertwined.
Each gives a sense of flight and aspiring mobility.
The overcoming of limitations, the buffer zone to
exist and become simultaneously.

By Cara E. Moore © 2005

PARALLEL WORLDS

The world of the homeless is violent world,
not unlike the one left behind.
A homeless person is like a shadow
moving against the intensity of daylight.

The porthole between worlds is a gate on one-side
 and a brick wall on the other.
Both worlds co-exist in the same boundaries.

Time wanes and ebbs for the homeless.
Daytime hours are for walking and
searching for the footholds over the wall.

Night time is for check-ins and staking a space to rest
and wash away the grime and despair.

By Cara E. Moore © 1992

LULLABY

I listen to the sounds you make
and see the wonder of your existence.

I see you as a baby listening to
the sounds of speech and feeling stirred. Knowing
that by concentrating on those sounds, was your
introduction into its world.

A mother's voice,
a wafting melody of comfort.
In the closeness of a heart's beating,
rocked and mixed with creamy warmth.

The nuance of undefined images, of things felt. Each
sensation mingled and indistinguishable.
Then the slipping away into the welcomed darkness, to await
the pang of the impulses of being alive.

By Cara E. Moore © 1987

Child in Crib, Cara E. Moore ©1997

A WRITER'S LOCKET

Writing is like a secret locket
Hidden underneath my outer-clothes.
My fingers touch the formed keys
Of the typewriter in a transferring motion.

The locket's presence focuses
My mind – picturing order
Onto the white rolled canvas.
I view images recalled,
Listen to the utterance of sounds,
Linking and piecing together
The fitting individual components.

In glimpses, when completed,,
The locket's contents are shared,
Some of its mystery revealed.

By Cara E. Moore © 1987

BUFFER ZONE

A buffer zone is a space in which to resolve conflict. A
room of one's own
whether in mind or actuality.
Away from the constant awareness of time,
and the slipping away of opportunity.

Without reflection and a sense of who one is, the
measured ticking away is a source of stress. An
assortment of needs and wants to be met.
All things can't be done; a choice has to be made.

Frustration, unhappiness, emptiness, loneliness,
are symptoms of a lack of completeness in the psyche.
Stress caused by shoving together ill-fitting pieces.
Long-term, these opposing forces are destructive. We
struggle to break-free, revolt, looking for an image to
reflect the needs of our individuality.

A balance is needed to insure a healthy lifestyle.
Relaxation and contentment result in well-being.
Hobbies, exercise, entertainment, daydreaming,
all serve as a place away to reflect, a chance to
step-back and observe, with objectivity the
direction of our forward linear existence.

Past hurts, disappointments, love lost, all
impede our perception of forward motion.
Friends, family, beliefs, accomplishments,
the steps taken to obtain our dreams and become
who we perceive we would like to be, heal us.

By Cara E. Moore © 1989

DENIAL

The reality is oppressive, as is the situation.
Yes, there was hope and understanding,
But not inside me, I couldn't understand.
The disparity of the realities too great.

I existed on a different plane for a long time,
Accepting the unacceptable, bearing the unbearable,
"just for a short while" that lasted for years.
Fear and pain were my constant companions.
Pain for a loss I never had in actuality, a myth.

Denial makes pain bearable,
But like a dam, it has its limits.
Pain is like water, heavy, even in small volumes.
Weary from the burden, I seek a haven.

I look and see the driftwood of my dreams along
The shore, I wade towards them out of the swift current.
I salvage and collect the remnants of my existence.
I am alive and that is all that is required,
The only pre-requisite needed for being.

Mourning has its place, it fulfills a need,
But not as a way of life, a career, an obsession.
There comes a time when the self-preserving nature of
Denial becomes an obstacle.

Walking away is another form of self-preservation,
It too can become a way of life. Yet it serve a purpose.
It is a stepping towards the road to reality,
A continuing towards the future as opposed to
Dwelling at crossroads of what might have been,
Should have been, imagined, but never existed.

We create the tone of our lives by our actions,
Our thoughts, the people who surround us, all
Of this creates the environment for our being.

By Cara E. Moore © 2005

CURRENTS WITHIN

My emotions are like the waves of the sea,
Ever churning and restless. Seemingly having no beginning
And no end. Each emotion is a continuance of the one before.
Each building up to form a tide that washes over me
And then retreats into the horizon; Giving life to the next
surging tide.

By Cara E. Moore © 1982

BREEZE

A breeze is
a soft caress on a hot day. Like a
hand, running its Fingers
through one's hair. A
breeze gives
The trees a chance to stretch.
The clouds gently float by,
Escorted by a breeze.
This cool sensation
Relieves tension,
And gives a feeling of freedom.
The wind of a breeze
Sings a wailing lullaby.
A breeze is
a refreshing tonic
for a blue day.

By Cara E. Moore ©1982

SHACKLED MEDITATION

A prison is a boundary between oneself and the outside world.
This boundary can be either man-made or mind-made;
Although there are No tangible walls, this prison
Has the strength of a fortress.
This castle's moat is a bottomless pit that
Surrounds it on all sides.
Escape is very difficult.
How does one escape from one's own mind
And not flee to another stronger confinement?

By Cara E. Moore ©1982

BURNISHED CHRISTMAS MEMORIES

The Christmas tree lights shine like tiny lighthouses
Against a sea of green branches. Decorations
clinging to fingers Protruding from the limbs. The
musty smell of annual treasures saved
To clothe the towering figure of the forest.
The presents are piled under the tree
In the tradition of the Magi
Each package containing a burnished memory that will
Linger long after the original gift is gone.

By Cara E. Moore ©1985

THE FALLEN TREE

Like a tree that has fallen in the forest
The sound of which no ear hears.
The cry of anguish.
The cutting and splinting of the whole.
The ultimate gouge of non-existence.

By Cara E. Moore © 1987

Fairy Stump, Cara E. Moore © 1987

HEART REALITY

Isolation of the heart is an alienation.
A detachment of our humanity, in our
empathic reasoning of motivations.
There is a need to know why in the context
of interactions with the cast of people who
influence and are part of our lives.

What is the meaning? Motivation of actions?
Politics? Beliefs? Belonging?
All these things bind us and separate us.
To live without feeling, to respond.
To act, disregarding human feelings,
alienates us from each other, creates
hostility, a need to resist.

A voice from the heart.
A source of reality, says,
"Wait, What is this? What does this mean?"
The heart views actions, words, reactions,
with an empathic protectiveness towards
our humanity. A feeling.
Acceptable or unacceptable.
We decide based on how we feel.

By Cara E. Moore © 1994

ABOUT THE AUTHOR

Cara E. Moore is a writer, poet and playwright who writes for Newspapers, Magazines and Internet sites, and whose play, The Healing won an honorable mention in the 1996 Writer's Digest Playwright Competition. Horizon's Place And Time Meet is Cara E. Moore's first collection of Poetry. She has given workshops in Poetry, and had a number of her poems published in poetry journals and featured in art galleries and events.

Review: Horizon's Place and Time meet by Cara E. Moore, published by the author. Poems that display integrity in their questioning of the big issues of mankind and the small moments of individuality. The voice is clear, crisp and direct. A first collection that has an accompanying c.d. Seventh Quarry, Summer Issue

www.ingramcontent.com/pod-product-compliance
Lightning Source LLC
Chambersburg PA
CBHW061349040426
42444CB00011B/3159